Disorders of the Blood

Disorders of the Blood

Leah Kaminsky

PUNCHER & WATTMANN

First published in 2024
Published by Puncher & Wattmann
PO Box 279
Waratah NSW 2298

info@puncherandwattmann.com

NATIONAL
LIBRARY
OF AUSTRALIA

A catologue record for this book is available from The National Library of Australia.

ISBN   9781923099364

Cover design by Maia Loeffler

Printed by Lightning Source International

Disorders of the Blood

Leah Kaminsky

*Title from Disorders of the Blood – by L.E.H. Whitby & C.J.C. Britton. Published by J&A Churchill Ltd, London 1939.

For Johanan, Alon, Ella & Maia – my all

'Our blood is time.'

Anne Michaels (Miner's Pond)

Contents

I: Disorders
of the Blood

Acute Haemorrhage

His body trickles out of itself
as she stands slightly stooped
watching his blood congeal
this moment of separation
a huge, irredeemable mistake
yet, from today, she will have peace

Years since she bled
she remembers a time
his body was home
sweat and bare flesh
he holds her hand
between icy palms

Now, together again
in daylight dreams and mist
she watches him
his mind still hungry for life
eyes begging her to speak
of something he can't recall

their first kiss
a chorus of jackals in the valley
the neighbour singing arias in the shower
bulbuls screeching in the pine
the blue-crimson thread of veins
woven across her thighs

Have you noticed

The way the valves — and their sorority of tangled strings —
flap like Dante's shades as you probe them under the gaze of
theatre lights, on their way down to hell
as though they were the only ones
left on this Earth?

The way the arteries in their sclerosed casing, eccentric layers of
stiffness, resist in disbelief. The avuncular surgeon coaxing them
like a child who will not move. But blood will ooze, peaceably crimson
in its trough. Flaring vermillion for a moment.

The way the fig is down to its skeleton
winter stripping the maple of its clothes
and the smell of rain before it falls, like sensing death
before it grips the trees, the moment, the heart.

Night always comes. And trees grow. And rain falls.
And then it stops. Nurses pull a blanket over the solitude. And
down in the morgue, the patient lies in naked awe as
time plays like a cat over her stilled breast

In Memoriam

What is a body, if not grace?
time worn, a book that can be read
a road map left so quietly by the dead
Legs that bore the weight of years
memory carved like etchings into skin
silken strands of wisdom line the heart

What is a man but specimen?
his name cleaved from the shell
that carried him through life
flesh, a rental car that drove him home
the not alive watch us through their lens
of time, waiting for the moment
when we gather them to us
to stand around them face to face and weep

Like children wading on the shores of lakes
we gaze upon the bodies of the dead
not knowing just how deep they plunge
we dive like birds to open up the wound
and glimpse beyond the privacy of death
into the very wellspring of our lives

Let us speak then to the dead
thank them for their whitened bones
that galloped over fields of hay
and waltzed across the room by night
now dust has settled on the lids
of eyes that saw soft summer's light of day
and ears that heard the creaking of a door
strong hands that cradled infants, planted trees

Beyond the firm umbrella of their flesh
follow quiet raindrops back in time
above and skyward bound
each drop returns to cloud
each cloud dissolving slowly into air
and air to space, with everything beyond

The dead enter our lives and trace
their memory stamped on teacups, rings and bears
paintings, vases, tables, chairs
we close their book
tears bathed in sacred space
What is a body, if not grace?

Hymn for the Flies I Just Sprayed

I'm running out of lifetime
—Yehuda Amichai

A buzzing chorus of black
zigzag around the kitchen light
plummet toward each other
collide and drop to the floor
spinning wildly in their dance

ghosts of wispy memory
invade the scene
huddled together by the stove
whispering, hovering
around the edges of my life

I wish them gone
end their shadowy nothing
and straight away, regretful
chase their graying bodies
as they leave

When I close my eyes
that final night
breathe myself in
and disappear
will they be waiting in the wings?

In Transit: Intensive Care

he loved in vain
his heart, an empty bag now, suspended
in the airport of his chest
shocked
drugged
frozen
the flight information screen showing
a runway of skipped beats
veins cloy to guide him back
onto the tarmac, homeward bound
indifferent valves lock
in preparation for departure
the crew wears scrubs
hands inside blue gloves
serving up ice on a tray
in emergency, plastic tubes
will drop down from the heavens

at home, his letterbox
    fills with advertisements
        from undertakers
            fighting for his corpse

Death Watch

Blood is charged with longing.
—Saul Bellow, *More Die of Heartbreak*

My father is making his way to the cemetery
fingering his wounds
as he watches game shows on TV

Shadows fall
aortic arch, vena cava, carotids
bloated with sluggish sap

Meanwhile, life has come to grab me
running along on clay feet
showing off its dazzling hues

I am busy with the living
while he is ravaged
by his ghosts

Decades later, I begin to see
the old woman, hair white
beckoning me to come

Time perhaps, to fill a few more years
swim between the flags
before drowning in illness

Cancer, Dementia, Arrythmia
Emphysema, Stroke, Septicaemia
Rock, Paper, Scissors.

Night Duty, Ward 8 East (Oncology)

Deliberately going into the darkness, and slowly drawing himself after
— D.H. Lawrence. Snake

soon it will lunge forward
emerge from itself
black eyeballs swivelling in their sockets
so hungry, it swallows its own tail

you could call it a journey inward
this devouring of a life
tied up in a Caduceus knot
dried out liars, thieves, alchemy
only to be sold at some night market
as a key chain to a tourist
who bargained for more

I remember the photos
China's tallest man, 7ft 8in
shaking the hand of
China's smallest man, 2ft 5in
and the woman with 250 grandchildren
who won the war

the snake slides down
in search of an obtuse trail
erasing any evidence it was ever really there

Music might help you

for Alex Skovron

when you die
the Messiah won't come
the birds won't sing

the dissonance of machines
beeping the rhythm of your heart
accompany you out from this world
they are the purgatory before Hell

it's the grace notes that linger
the melody of a child's laugh, a cat's purr,
words of love, whispered
by someone from your past

a rabbit's stomp
the bubbling of soup in the pot
an old friend at the end of the phone
ringing to say goodbye

these melodies
may help you in the end
the fanfare passing
from heart to heart

Are We There Yet?

Heading into empty space, words packed tightly in the trunk
those hollow incantations of narrative and noise
I carry with me snacks of memory and regret
three toddlers singing wildly in the back, no longer there
I'm in a hurry though, bound as I am
for who-knows-where

Amichai and Olds my trusty guides
I've left the empty weight of home behind
the cat curled up inside itself, asleep
the smell of onions absent in the air
other people's children in my street
silence a new tongue I've learnt to speak

I kissed the cherry dress goodbye before I left
a flag of childhood tucked away from sight
I cruise along the road, dead forests line the way
I've never learnt to read a map, coordinates confuse
North, the other side of South, I'm speeding fast towards myself
each mile draws deeper still to somewhere else

We are endangered species, you and I
spring turned to autumn, sun grown cold
white frost reflected in the moon like bones
I chant your name and howl the ache of past
my heart, a leaden bank vault filled with dreams
hoards years of photos, books and toys
three dogs, five cats, two turtles buried there
too many ghostlet rabbits gone to count

Drunk with the dead, I crash into the waning of my life
the ice, the heat, the rain from which I race
and waiting at the other end, there's you
your empty arms a shadow of embrace

II: Chronic Bleeding

The McGill Pain Questionnaire

a priestly litany
trying to translate pain
back to her
as the body's news

Describe it
        she is silent; eyes speak the truth

How long has it been there?
        fingers the glass beads of her necklace

Sharp or dull?
        grammar and syntax will not do

Worse with movement?
        her spine has hasped and hooped

Aggravated by food?
        whispering weariness of fallen stone

Constant?
        pounces like a feral cat

On a scale of 1-10?
        a thousand, a million, a universe

Is it quivering, shooting, drilling, stabbing, cutting, pinching,
cramping, crushing, burning, stinging, blinding, piercing,
excruciating?

the answer lies in howled vowels

The Origin of Cells of the Blood

Early in foetal life the liver and spleen take over the function of blood cell formation *

if there is laughter in the womb
then, sometime between
the first cell
and labour
the punchline
is forgotten

* *Disorders of the Blood* – by L.E.H. Whitby & C.J.C. Britton. Published by J&A Churchill Ltd, London 1939.

In the Children's Ward with my Son

For Alon

hard to keep my eyes off the chart
the drip, the staccato line on the monitor
beside his bed

hard to keep my eyes off the needle
the tourniquet, his blood
dripping out from a vein

hard to keep my eyes off his legs
white and withered
his body falling into itself

hard to keep my eyes off his eyes
my nails digging into the armrests
of the red vinyl chair

he weeps quietly
beside me on the bed
I am doctor turned mother now

holding his hand
as they stab a needle into his back
clear fluid dripping into glass vials

at night I glare at the scans
his spine a spray of bones
like leftovers from the sabbath trout

hard not to peek at results
to finally know
what I do not want to know

hard not to stare at the pompous white coats
search the eyes of colleagues
turned enemy today

hard to hope for his future
without searching the shadows of my past

Mourning Rounds, Pandemic

Blurry light of morning
sneaks around frayed edges of the blind
my glasses lie abandoned
an out of focus world feels safer
than the day that waits
In the half-dark I steal this time
to sift through detritus of dreams
these precious moments curled into myself

Before the kettle boils
before the toast and jam
the cats demand their milk
the shower washes off the mask of sleep
this greedy generosity to self
birdsong pushing through the cracks
before putting on my scrubs, a gown, a smile
the sick, the old, the ancient waiting
in the wings, as I shout and crawl and cry
it's been thirty years of listening to
this play-track of the ones who'll die

Friends call to say they're bored
Twitter claps for me each day
a hero in this pantomime of war, they say
my mother wore a Star of David
on her withered breast
the cusp of war approaching feels mundane
This time, when all are folded in themselves
falling onto swords, our bloody tears
will be too late to save the rest
daily forecasts - nightmares yet to come
Saul's punishment for pride seems just desserts

Still, I'll step out in the world
talk and listen, argue, yell, cajole
check, read, call, counsel, soothe
tremble, clean, debride, control
the verbs of daily grind
hide my howls, behind
the mask donated back to me
That muted light of waking
washing onto shoreless depths of day
long-evaporated dreams
of reverie and screams

Home Visit with Duck

Continents of stains float
on his blue-check shirt
while a feathered lunatic
chases me across the floor

Don't mind her. She's toothless, Doc

Roll up one sleeve
to check his pressure
as Ray stabs a fork into
a plate of cold baked beans

I try not think too much about dying, Doc

Listen to his heart
he's chewing slowly
pushing food from one side
of his plate to the other

Only wanna die once, Doc

Takes an empty beer bottle
filled with milk
covers it with a rubber teat
and feeds the black lamb waiting at the door

Don't wanna die a thousand deaths a day, Doc

Pet cemetery at the bottom of the garden
little lives grown large in Ray's care
the duck waddles outside and jumps
into a basket, eyeing me as I leave

Onion Days

yom asal, yom basal
one day honey, one day onions
—Arabic saying

tears of a tree
decay and fall
to be trampled on by a man
trudging through his marriage

crude bunglings of apologies
everyday imperfections
burnt toast, frayed seams
held up like dirty underwear

his only grievance, her silence
reading novels in bed
his words shuffle and change
the penalty, other men

dishes pile up
a traffic of ants over cups
words should be useful
not land like dead leaves

On Becoming a Fridge

'Women should dress in white, like all domestic appliances'
—Formula One CEO 2005

It happens suddenly
late evening
during the replay
> when he demands a beer

she opens the fridge
runs her hand over
cool, shiny enamel
> and slips away

time flows quickly
in freeze-thaw cycles
coils absorb body heat
> her skin frozen hard

when she doesn't answer
he lurches to the kitchen
searching in the chiller
> for another Foster's lager

something hisses at him
she could shed some light on things
watch him reach into her tray
> then slam herself shut

unseeing
he yells for her to come
as she rolls towards him quietly
> what to do now?

kill him with the weight of years
then slowly cruise back to her corner
turn on snooze cycle
        and purr like a cat?

no, for him to be dead is not revenge enough
better to freeze his beer

III: Spleen & Marrow

The New Hell in Three Acts

from a Nazi propaganda film about the Warsaw Ghetto

ACT I:

In the *Novi Azazel* Theatre
she becomes Scheherazade
for an audience forced to laugh
at 1,001 lies

sole star, how does she recite
her lines of darkness
knowing argent-lidded eyes
will soon turn dull?

she clutches a rose
 who ever saw a flower?
pours a glass of wine
 we barely had water

ACT II:

sweetest lady of the stage
outside, a child hugs the wall
watching rats tiptoe
over his mother's corpse

ACT III:

a goodly place, a goodly time
until another night in night
when telling the untellable
makes even silence vanish

CRITIC'S REVIEW:

an encyclopaedia of facts
a decade later, becomes a tale
fifty years on, a poem
and tomorrow, will only be a word

First Bruise

For Maia

the Tree Care guys back their truck
into the old wattle
half-crack a bough
its bark paper-thin
air suddenly frantic with bees

yellow tresses fall
branches in crucified shock
weeds and trees and grass
abandon their eager greenness
to the haemorrhaging of sap

my daughter, suspended midair
above the trampoline
blond curls petrified in the sun
sees her tree dismembered
at night, blossom cries itself to sleep

Jeder Engel Ist Schrecklich

Every angel is terrifying.
—Rilke. *Duino Elegies*

great grandfather soiled the family tree
lifted his penis high in the air
and peed on its trunk
the stump of my mother

great aunt had young lovers
and hidden amongst the foliage of time
stories lurked in cupboards
behind the smiling faces of fading photos

three sisters wear each other's clothes
while their mother rocks her lovers
in the marital bed, the dead father's photo
swinging in time on its nail

we are of bastard stock it seems
look in the mirror myself
and see the Cossack rape
full moon face, blonde hair, blue eyes

mother silent over winter snow
and frigid with her frosty breath
covers her mouth with a scarf
so we cannot see the chilling truth

the dead sclerose my dreams
hated oddities, they fall out
like unwanted fetuses
curled up inside their beginnings

Colours My Mother Taught Me

I learned black when I was six
the hole she fell into most days
wisps of smoke clouding the kitchen

I learned red when I was ten
photos of bleeding bodies slumped
under the shade of pines

I learned green when I was fifteen
saw a tall man outside our house
standing in the damp of night

Blue came when I was twenty-one
tracing the stiffened veins
on the back of her hand

At fifty I am starting to learn about light
its refraction, reflection, distortion, gleam
and how grey always hovers in the wings

The Languages I Know

Love
    Caged silence. Tongue tied. Straddling oceans, continents.

Hate
    Quick blood of chaos. Towers of babble. Lashing microworlds.

Fear
    Rolled up. Trembling cornered prey. Waits for a fatal bite.

Child
    Wayward folly. Feathery afternoons. Smile, blonde curls, fluttering heart.

At Fifty

I wear mostly black nowadays
some say it flatters
after forty-eight years
I am still reaching out my hand
to reclaim my half-eaten toast
from Kimmy the dog

he stands at the back door
of our house on Allison Road
a black and white blur
friendly eyes gone wild
as I find myself suddenly, too soon in life
regretting love gone wrong

Lipczynska Forest, Poland, 1942

to fall into snow and sleep
frozen in a white cast
that covers this bloodied earth
remember nothing

this is the border
of the badlands
where God was looking
somewhere else

in their hideout
strangled by her nephew
my great grandmother's last breath
was a cough

the sound of Gestapo boots
marching overhead

Blood Libel

blood clots
melt into time
bleeding goes the way of clouds
disappearing into a red sky

no one questions truth
gazing upon those
fuelled by the mere shadow
of a bruise

while heaven sleeps
they gather outside the town
whispers turn
to rampage

drain the lifeblood
of cattle, sheep, fowl
before rubbing salt into
bloodshot eyes

an ardour of fury
the beast
with its ancient lust
quivers in the crawling light of day

Now I am Six

so I think I'll be six now for ever and ever
—A. A. Milne, *Now We Are Six*

I remember Punch and Judy
the red velvet curtain hiding the puppeteer.
Punch hit Judy over the head
with a wooden stick

How they fought
each time Judy
bouncing back
for more

I remember the laughter of kids
as Judy begged him to stop
I wanted to get up and show them
the man behind all her tears

but I froze to my spot
in the front row
Birthday Girl
in her white party dress

I remember the ash from mother's cigarette
flicked onto my leg
and the tears and the sting
the look in her eyes

Hauntings

unmoored absences
loiter around the house
hanging from ceilings
leaning against walls

domestic haints
stranded in musty corners
overburdened ruins
carrying the weight of time

fractious conjurers
disillusioned with death
they pull memories
from backpacks full of thwarted desire

longing for whisky
a decent pickle
one night of Polish rummy
the return of spring

some days you don't notice them
deaf to their siren calls
able to ignore those mirror eyes
staring back

other days they swallow you whole
drowning in decades of pain
what was once unbreachable
becomes an unfathomable rift

barely a footnote in history
their only claim to fame
a chunk of grey marble
embellished with their names

an archaeologist might lead
a salvage operation
searching for remnants
of their vanished world

even absence disappears
a wave washed up
onshore for a moment
swallowed back into the depths

God could not be everywhere, so he made mothers

Yiddish proverb

walk backwards, mother
along the driveway
through the front door
put down the basket, keys
sit at the kitchen table again
and light another cigarette
stare at smoke clouds in the air
do not let me wait so long
for you to leave me alone
holding back the guileless promise
of a small child

come back, mother
into this god-forsaken house
unlock that bedroom door
the flames rushing to engulf
as I dance, my moo-moo dress
with the white tassel trim
slumped on the floor
what the body endures
memory tries to forget
six decades of flesh
silent in its pain

follow these lines, mother
you left long before you were gone
could not be everywhere
could not be anywhere

The Universal Recipient: AB Positive

for Ella

she is a rare type
anyone can give her blood
and she will take it in
never rejecting the ghosts

and through my torrid insomniac night
I arrive into the imagined memory
of some darkened hospital corridor
in some place she's never been

I recognise the thin curve of her body
stretched out on a gurney
half turned away from me
as I hover in the ether of maternal angst

I poison her with cursed imagination
the steady drip feed
of murdered relatives
staring out from unmarked graves

the digital clock bleeds
03:33 flows into 04:46
as I count the wraiths of time
transfused into her vein

In a moment of cowardice
or shame, I let go
of all the stories thrust upon
her languid frame

wake to the smell
of burning toast
the tea poured back into her life
needing to become its own

IV: Coagulation

The Wind Keeps Forgetting

the wind, in its hurry to get somewhere

doesn't see the spiderling wake at dawn
    carefully climb in concentric silk
around the spokes of its webs
    weaving crisscross to and fro
fastening itself in the middle
    to wait

the wind, in its hurry to get somewhere

collects twigs, dry leaves
    Snickers wrappers, torn Target catalogues
wears them like fancy dress
    over its invisible, shifting form
as if to laugh at the world
    so busy trying to hold on to its own centre

The Taxonomy of Ghosts

Linnaeus was in reality a poet who happened to become a naturalist.
—August Strindberg

The bench on which I sit
in Melbourne's Botanical Gardens
has a plaque in memory of *Marjory Pearce*

everything here has a name
Coprosma x'kikii
Sophora Tetraptera

a black water hen
Gallinula ventralis
searches for *Lumbricus terrestris*

children roll on the *Buchloe dachyloides*
their father calling them to come
Sasha! Tommy!

a couple kiss passionately
under the *British tulip oak*
Oh, *Michael*, don't!

Bill, the photographer, trails a bride
and two white *Samoyeds* on a leash
Smile, *Jenny*, darling

Argiope aurantia spins its story
Columba livia sits in a *Norfolk pine*
Larus occidentalis preening on the lake

clouds, sky, breeze
birdsong, helicopter, poem
all labelled

The bench in these gardens
has me sitting beside my ghosts

busy memorialising the nameless
while trying to name the un-nameable

Upgraded

The species is listed as critically endangered by the Australian government but was upgraded to extinct on the International Union for the Conservation of Nature list
—*The Guardian* 10/12/2022

Mountain Mist Frog
once covered two-thirds of the wet tropics
last seen April 1990
in the rainforest at Thornton Peak

six centimetres long
greyish brown
black spots on its back
now silent

And would you like fries with that?

The Many Faces of Evening

She is non-judgemental
apolitical in the main
doesn't give a hoot for niceties

Bathing in dragon's blood
stealth is her strength
sits in ambush, pouncing like a wildcat

Raining down oblivion
fine as a cobweb
hard as stone

Listen

Birdsong
the dog lapping at the water bowl
in the laundry, where the
washing machine beeps insistently
come and hang out the load
Somewhere
a good man mows the lawn
a crow laughs
pebbles crackle under a shoe

now the dog scrapes its old teeth
against a dead cow's hip
who, a week ago
chomped at hay
grinding as it snorted
and swished its tail
moaning deep and mournful songs
into the metal bars of its stall

Worms are the Words

oozing through thoughts
wriggling around the rim
of the compost
slimy and spineless

unseeing in their ugly beauty
they crawl out from the dirt
wind their way over rotten fruit
lead by their blindness
following an inner trail
driven by hunger
maddened by the sun

A mad bull & a migratory bird

Hackles raised, nostrils flaring
it lunges to its death
impaling itself
onto the sword hidden behind a red cape
hardly a fight
more a readying for martyrdom
death from fury at humankind
in all its decorated, trinketed stupidity

Flapping of feathers
starts several days before flight
migration imprinted
hard-wired into the anxiety of preparation
the foreknowledge of flying or dying
restlessness
before the escape
the search for sky

Homeostasis Chart, Midnight

Emergency Admission

Patient: M. Earth

Ward: 9 South

DOB: 4.543 billion years ago

Differential Diagnosis: generalised systemic collapse - For Investigation

Observations:

Temp
59.4 ° C
Vasodilation to cool down, allowing more heat to escape through the skin.

Toxins
Reached dangerous levels. Check to ensure they are being excreted.

BP
Unacceptable levels of pressure. Heart racing.

pH
pH levels unbalanced Acidification. Lungs pushing more CO_2 out of diaphragm.

Glucose levels
Elevated. Too much sweetness becomes intolerable.

Prognosis:
Uncertain

Acknowledgments

My deepest gratitude to David Musgrave, publisher at Puncher & Wattmann for his belief in my work. Thanks to Alicia Sometimes, Cate Kennedy, Peter Straus, Alex Skovron, Kent MacCarter, Lesley Smith, Ryan Jefferies, Professor Michael Hulse and the late Professor Donald Singer, for their encouragement and support.

Poems in this collection have previously appeared in *The Fractured Self Anthology (UWAP)*, *Hippocrates Anthology of the Heart*, *IP Anthology*, *Hope anthology (ACU)*, *Evening Paper*, *Cordite Review*.

Acute Haemorrhage was commissioned and exhibited at the *Blood* exhibition: Blood & Science (Science Gallery, Melbourne University, 2017) & published in *The Fractured Self Anthology* (UWAP). It was also commended in the 2016 Health Poetry Prize, Canberra University.

Have you noticed was published in *Hippocrates Anthology of the Heart* 2017

In Memoriam was commended in the Hippocrates Prize for Poetry & Medicine, 2016. It was commissioned for the Melbourne University Donor's Thanksgiving Service and published in *The Fractured Self Anthology* (University of Western Australia Press)

Hymn for the flies I just sprayed was published in *IP Anthology* 2017

The McGill Pain Questionnaire was commended in the Hippocrates Poetry Prize 2017

In the children's ward with my son was shortlisted for the 2022 ACU Prize for Poetry. And published in *Hope Anthology* (ed Robert Carver & Margot Hillel), ACU 2022

Mourning Rounds, Pandemic was shortlisted in the ACU Prize for Poetry 2020.

The New Hell in Three Acts was published in *IP Anthology* 2017

First Bruise was published in *Evening Paper* Volume 1, September 2015. Centre for Narrative Practice, USA

Jeder Engel ist Schrecklich was published in *Cordite Review* 2012

The Wind Keeps Forgetting was published *in IP Anthology* 2017 & *The Fractured Self Anthology* (UWAP)

Some of these poems were written during a residency at the Brooklyn Morbid Anatomy Museum, NYC (2015) and at a Cove Park Fellowship, Scotland (2022), courtesy of the Bridge Awards and Varuna – the Writer's House.